Christian Home Library

A CALL TO MEDICAL EVANGELISM

AND

HEALTH EDUCATION

Ellen G. White

LS Company

ISBN: 978-1-0879-5764-7

Copyright ©2021

Content:

Foreword 9

A Call to Service 11

    The Compassion of Christ Revealed 11

    Divine Origin 12

    The Gospel of Health 12

    The Right Hand of the Gospel 12

    It Opens Doors 12

    The Work for Today 13

    An Early Call to Action—1867 13

    A Rallying Call in 1902 14

    The Call Repeated in 1907 14

    The Call of Today 14

    Zeal and Perseverance Required 15

    In Time of Persecution 15

    The Distinguishing Sign 15

    Ways Will Open 16

The Call of the Cities 17

    Companies of Workers 17

    Redeeming the Time 18

    A Mighty Movement 18

    Teach in Simplicity and Faith 18

    With Sympathy and Tenderness 18

    Divine Power Will Attend 19

Ways of Working 20

    A Door of Entrance to the Cities 20

    Organize for Harmonious Action 20

    The Church a Training School 21

    The Need for Consecrated Nurses 21

    Serve With Sanctified Understanding 22

Medical Missions in Every City 22

The City Mission and Training School 23

Training Under Competent Leaders 23

Laboring as God's Helping Hand 23

Self-supporting Workers 24

Hygienic Restaurants as Missionary Centers 24

To Supply Spiritual Food 24

Results of Consecrated Effort 25

Christian Help Work 26

Carrying the Gospel to the Poor 26

Helping the Helpless 27

A Witness to the Power of Christianity 28

Need of Greater Faith 28

Keeping Our Souls Alive 28

Use Your Humble Talent 29

An Expression of Gratitude 29

A Complete Ministry 31

The Physician as an Evangelist 31

The Minister as a Medical Missionary 31

Teaching Health Principles 32

The Missionary Nurse 32

Do Not Wait 33

Teaching Health Principles 34

Educate, Educate, Educate 34

Teach Skillfully 35

A Continual Reform Essential 35

Responsibility of Those Who Have Light 36

Thousands Eager to Learn 36

The Public to Be Deeply Stirred 36

Health Talks to Be Given 37

Physiology to Be Taught 37

Represented by Advance Principles 37

Education Better Than Miraculous Healing ... 38

When Prayer for Healing Is Presumption ... 38

Instruction in Diet by Evangelistic Workers ... 39

A Knowledge of Healthful Cookery ... 39

Simplicity in Cooking ... 39

Decision Without Narrow Conceit ... 40

The Temperance Work ... 41

Make Plain the Effects of Indulgence ... 42

Many May Be Saved From Degradation ... 42

Pledging to Total Abstinence ... 42

Responsibility of Parents ... 43

A Clear Testimony Needed ... 43

Co-operation Between Medical and Evangelistic Work ... 45

To Advance Together ... 45

Combined Teaching and Healing ... 45

The Advantages of Medical Workers ... 46

Medical and Evangelistic Work Bound Together 46

No Other Work So Successful 46

The Minister, the Physician, and the Bible Worker 47

There Must Be No Separation 47

Education for Medical Missionary Work 48

Equipment for Service 49

A Solemn Warning 49

The Only Medium for Character Building 50

Humility and Love 50

Meeting God at the Altar of Self-sacrifice 50

The Highest Service 51

Foreword

A clarion call to medical evangelism is due at this time. Thousands, yes, tens of thousands of people today are asleep to the condition of their spiritual and their physical health. They are far from the better way of life and do not sense their peril. Faithful watchmen are needed to point out the way of health and holiness.

The call to medical evangelism is first given Seventh-day Adventists in the example of Christ in his own ministry and in his gospel commission to the church. He "who went about doing good, healing all that were oppressed of the devil," showed that true evangelism comprehends ministry to physical needs as well as to spiritual.

The history of the Advent movement has been characterized by a dual ministry. Health and temperance work has always been a part of world evangelism. Many important reforms in healthful living are recognized as being closely interwoven with the Advent gospel message. Pointing the way to a full observance of God's law has included the recognition of the laws of health.

In the development of the medical missionary interests, institutions have been established and numerous educational centers and many training facilities have been provided for teaching the ways of right living and for fitting men and women to help others.

But again there rings in Adventist ears the command, "go out into the highways and hedges, and compel them to come in, that my house may be filled."

A forward step is imperative; a new note must be struck. Thousands of laymen must now hear and repeat the call to medical missionary evangelism. Hundreds of nurses who have had a thorough training in denominational sanitariums should engage in medical evangelism, and with some additional training they could be leaders in the work. Scores of young men should qualify to be lecturers. Physicians should sense fully their responsibility of imparting the message of health and temperance in talks and lectures in Adventist churches and before non-Adventist audiences in the great cities. Ministers should lead out as organizers and teachers of bands of young evangelists.

For the successful prosecution of this work, lecture materials, books on health and temperance, and instruction regarding the organization and conduct of health and home nursing classes have been provided. Those who take up this work should seek counsel and help from conference leaders.

The messenger of the Lord through her current books, Review and Herald articles, and manuscripts calls the entire church to medical evangelism. May the study of these stirring messages lead to a great advance movement among Seventh-day Adventists in medical missionary work and medical evangelism.

Chapter 1

A Call to Service

The Entering Wedge

I can see in the Lord's providences that the medical missionary work is to be a great entering wedge, whereby the diseased soul may be reached. —*Counsels on Health, 535.*

The evangelization of the world is the work that God has given to those who go forth in His name. They are to be colaborers with Christ, revealing to those ready to perish His tender, pitying love. God calls for thousands to work for Him, not by preaching to those who know the truth, going over and over the same ground, but by warning those who have never heard the last message of mercy. Work with a heart filled with an earnest longing for souls. Do medical missionary work. Thus you will gain access to the hearts of the people. The way will be prepared for more decided proclamation of the truth. You will find that relieving their physical suffering gives an opportunity to minister to their spiritual needs.

The Lord will give you success in this work, for the gospel is the power of God unto salvation, when it is interwoven with the practical life, when it is lived and practiced. The union of Christlike work for the body and Christlike work for the soul is the true interpretation of the gospel. —*An Appeal for the Medical Missionary College, pp. 14, 15.*

The Compassion of Christ Revealed

Medical missionary work brings to humanity the gospel of release from suffering. It is the pioneer work of the gospel. It is the gospel practiced, the compassion of Christ revealed. Of this work there is great need, and the world is open for it. God grant that the importance of medical missionary work shall be understood, and that new fields may be immediately entered. —*Medical Ministry, 239.*

Divine Origin

True medical missionary work is of heavenly origin. It was not originated by any person who lives. But in connection with this work we see so much which dishonors God that I am instructed to say, The medical missionary work is of divine origin and has a most glorious mission to fulfill. In all its bearings it is to be in conformity with Christ's work. Those who are workers together with God will just as surely represent the character of Christ as Christ represented the character of His Father while in this world. —*Medical Ministry, 24.*

The Gospel of Health

The principles of health reform are found in the Word of God. The gospel of health is to be firmly linked with the ministry of the Word. It is the Lord's design that the restoring influence of health reform shall be a part of the last great efforts to proclaim the gospel message. —*Medical Ministry, 259.*

As a means of overcoming prejudice and gaining access to minds, medical missionary work must be done, not in one or two places only, but in many places where the truth has not yet been proclaimed. We are to work as gospel medical missionaries, to heal the sin-sick souls by giving them the message of salvation. This work will break down prejudice as nothing else can. —*Testimonies for the Church 9:211.*

The Right Hand of the Gospel

Medical missionary work is the right hand of the gospel. It is necessary to the advancement of the cause of God. As through it men and women are led to see the importance of right habits of living, the saving power of the truth will be made known. Every city is to be entered by workers trained to do medical missionary work. As the right hand of the third angel's message, God's methods of treating disease will open doors for the entrance of present truth. —*Testimonies for the Church 7:59.*

It Opens Doors

The right hand is used to open doors through which the body may find entrance. This is the part the medical missionary work is to act. It is to largely prepare the way for the reception of the truth for this time. A body without hands is useless. In giving honor to the body, honor must also be given to the helping hands, which are agencies of such importance that without them the body can do nothing. Therefore the body which treats indifferently the right hand, refusing its aid, is able to accomplish nothing. —*Medical Ministry, 238.*

In every place the sick may be found, and those who go forth as workers for Christ should be true health reformers, prepared to give those who are sick the simple treatments that will relieve them, and then pray with them. Thus they will open the door for the entrance of the truth. The doing of this work will be followed by good results. —*Medical Ministry, 320.*

The Work for Today

Why has it not been understood from the Word of God that the work being done in medical missionary lines is a fulfillment of the scripture, "Go out quickly into the streets and lanes of the city, and bring in hither the poor, and the maimed, and the halt, and the blind.... The servant said, Lord, it is done as thou hast commanded, and yet there is room. And the lord said unto the servant, Go out into the highways and hedges, and compel them to come in, that my house may be filled."

This is a work that the churches in every locality, north and south and east and west, should do. The churches have been given the opportunity of answering this work. Why have they not done it? Someone must fulfill the commission. —*The Review and Herald, May 25, 1897.*

The Lord gave me great light on health reform. In connection with my husband, I was to be a medical missionary worker. I was to set an example to the church by taking the sick to my home and caring for them. This I have done, giving the women and children vigorous treatment.

I was also to speak on the subject of Christian temperance, as the Lord's appointed messenger. I engaged heartily in this work and spoke to large assemblies on temperance in its broadest and truest sense. —*The Review and Herald, July 26, 1906.*

An Early Call to Action—1867

I saw that the Lord was giving us an experience which would be of the highest value to us in the future in connection with His work.... I saw that God was fitting up my husband to engage in the solemn, sacred work of reform which He designs shall progress among His people.

It is important that instructions should be given by ministers in regard to living temperately. They should show the relation which eating, working, resting, and dressing sustain to health.

All who believe the truth for these last days have something to do in this matter. It concerns them, and God requires them to arouse and interest themselves in this reform. He will not be pleased with their course if they regard this question with indifference. —*Testimonies for the Church 1:618.*

A Rallying Call in 1902

We have come to a time when every member of the church should take hold of medical missionary work. The world is a lazar house filled with victims of both physical and spiritual disease. Everywhere people are perishing for lack of a knowledge of the truths that have been committed to us. The members of the church are in need of an awakening, that they may realize their responsibility to impart these truths. —*Testimonies for the Church 7:62.*

The Call Repeated in 1907

Medical missionary work is yet in its infancy. The meaning of genuine medical missionary work is known by but few. Why?— Because the Saviour's plan of work has not been followed. God's money has been misapplied. In many places practical, evangelistic, medical missionary work is being done, but many of the workers who should go forth as did the disciples are being collected together and held in a few places, as they have been in the past, notwithstanding the Lord's warning that this should not be. —*Special Testimonies, Series B, No. 8, p. 28.*

The Call of Today

The purest example of unselfishness is now to be shown by our medical missionary workers. With the knowledge and experience gained by practical work, they are to go out to give treatments to the sick. As they go from house to house, they will find access to many hearts. Many will be reached who otherwise would never have heard the gospel message. —*Counsels on Health, 538.*

A new element needs to be brought into the work. God's people must receive the warning and work for souls right where they are, for people do not realize their great need and peril. Christ sought the people where they were, and placed before them the great truths in regard to His kingdom. As He went from place to place, He blessed and comforted the suffering and healed the sick. This is our work. God would have us relieve the necessities of the destitute. The reason that the Lord does not manifest His power more decidedly is because there is so little spirituality among those who claim to believe the truth. —*Medical Ministry, 319.*

Zeal and Perseverance Required

Could I arouse our people to Christian effort, could I lead them to engage in medical missionary work with holy zeal and divine perseverance, not in a few places, but in every place, putting forth personal effort for those out of the fold, how grateful I should be! This is true missionary work. In some places it is attended with little success, apparently; but again, the Lord opens the way, and signal success attends the effort. Words are spoken which are as nails fastened in a sure place. Angels from heaven co-operate with human instrumentalities, and sinners are won to the Saviour. —*Medical Ministry, 256.*

In Time of Persecution

As religious aggression subverts the liberties of our nation, those who would stand for freedom of conscience will be placed in unfavorable positions. For their own sake, they should, while they have the opportunity, become intelligent in regard to disease, its causes, prevention, and cure. All those who do this will find a field of labor anywhere. There will be suffering ones, plenty of them, who will need help, not only among those of our own faith, but largely among those who know not the truth. The shortness of time demands an energy that has not been aroused among those who claim to believe the present truth. —*Counsels on Health, 506.*

The Distinguishing Sign

True sympathy between man and his fellow men is to be the sign distinguishing those who love and fear God from those who are unmindful of His law. How great the sympathy that Christ expressed in coming to this world to give His life a sacrifice for a dying world! His religion led to the doing of genuine medical missionary work. He was a healing power. "I will have mercy, and not sacrifice," He said. This is the test that the great Author of truth used to distinguish between true religion and false. God wants His medical missionaries to act with the tenderness and compassion that Christ would show were He in our world. —*Medical Ministry, 251.*

How slow men are to understand God's preparation for the day of His power. He works today to reach hearts in the same way that He worked when Christ was upon this earth. In reading the Word of God, we see that Christ brought medical missionary work into His ministry. Cannot our eyes be opened to discern Christ's methods? Cannot we understand the commission He gave to His disciples and to us?

The world must have an antidote for sin. As the medical missionary works intelligently to relieve suffering and save life, hearts are softened. Those who are helped are filled with gratitude. As the medical missionary works upon the body, God works upon the heart. —*Manuscript 58, 1901.*

Ways Will Open

In the future our work is to be carried forward in self-denial and self-sacrifice even beyond that which we have seen in past years. God desires us to commit our souls to Him, that He may work through us in manifold ways. I feel intensely over these matters. Brethren, let us walk in meekness and lowliness of mind and put before our associates an example of self-sacrifice. If we do our part in faith, God will open ways before us now undreamed of. —*Manuscript 12, 1913.*

We shall see the medical missionary work broadening and deepening at every point of its progress, because of the inflowing of hundreds and thousands of streams, until the whole earth is covered as the waters cover the sea. —*Medical Ministry, 317.*

Chapter 2

The Call of the Cities

Who Are Called

From the light that God has given me, I know that His cause today is in great need of the living representative of Bible truth. The ordained ministers, alone, are not equal to the task. God is calling Bible workers, and other consecrated laymen of varied talent who have a knowledge of present truth, to consider the needs of the unwarned cities. There should be one hundred believers actively engaged in personal missionary work where now there is but one. Time is rapidly passing. There is much work to be done before satanic opposition shall close up the way. Every agency must be set in operation, that present opportunities may be wisely improved. —*Medical Ministry, 248.*

Companies of Workers

During the night of February 27 (1910), a representation was given me in which the unworked cities were presented before me as a living reality, and I was plainly instructed that there should be a decided change from past methods of working. For months the situation has been impressed on my mind, and I urged that companies be organized and diligently trained to labor in our important cities. These workers should labor two and two, and from time to time all should meet together to relate their experiences, to pray and to plan how to reach the people quickly, and thus, if possible, redeem the time. —*Manuscript 21, 1910.*

The importance of making our way in the great cities is still kept before me. For many years the Lord has been urging upon us this duty, and yet we see but comparatively little accomplished in our great centers of population. If we do not take up this work in a determined manner, Satan will multiply difficulties which will not be easy to surmount. We are far behind in doing the work that should have been done in these long-neglected cities. The work will now be more difficult than it would have been a few years ago. But if we take up the work in the name of the Lord, barriers will be broken down, and decided victories will be ours.

In this work physicians and gospel ministers are needed. We must press our petitions to the Lord and do our best, pressing forward with all the energy possible to make an opening in the large cities. Had we in the past worked after the Lord's plans, many lights would be shining brightly that are going out. —*Medical Ministry, 301, 302.*

Redeeming the Time

The terrible disasters that are befalling great cities ought to arouse us to intense activity in giving the warning message to the people in these congested centers of population while we still have an opportunity. The most favorable time for the presentation of our message in the cities has passed by. Sin and wickedness are rapidly increasing; and now we shall have to redeem the time by laboring all the more earnestly. —*Medical Ministry, 310.*

A Mighty Movement

There is no change in the messages that God has sent in the past. The work in the cities is the essential work for this time. When the cities are worked as God would have them, the result will be the setting in operation of a mighty movement such as we have not yet witnessed. —*Medical Ministry, 304.*

The medical missionary work is a door through which the truth is to find entrance to many homes in the cities. —*Counsels on Health, 556.*

Teach in Simplicity and Faith

The Lord is speaking to His people at this time, saying, Gain an entrance into the cities, and proclaim the truth in simplicity and in faith. Introduce no strange doctrine into your message, but speak the simple words of the gospel of Christ, which young and old can understand. The unlearned as well as the educated are to comprehend the truths of the third angel's message, and they must be taught in simplicity. If you would approach the people acceptably, humble your hearts before God and learn His ways.

With Sympathy and Tenderness

We shall gain much instruction for our work from a study of Christ's methods of labor and His manner of meeting the people. In the gospel story we have the record of how He worked for all classes, and of how as He labored in cities and towns, thousands were drawn to His side to hear His teaching. The words of the Master were clear and distinct and were spoken in sympathy and tenderness. They carried with them the assurance that here was truth. It was the simplicity and earnestness with which Christ labored and spoke that drew so many to Him.

The Great Teacher laid plans for His work. Study these plans. We find Him traveling from place to place, followed by crowds of eager listeners. When He could, He would lead them away from the crowded cities to the quiet of the country. Here He would pray with them and talk to them of eternal truths.

The sympathy that Christ ever expressed for the physical needs of His hearers won many a response to the truths He sought to teach. Was not the gospel message of deepest importance to that company of five thousand people who for hours had followed Him and hung upon His words? Many had never before heard truths such as they listened to on that occasion. Yet Christ's desire to teach them spiritual truths did not make Him indifferent to their physical needs. —*Medical Ministry, 299.*

Divine Power Will Attend

Let many now ask, "Lord, what wilt thou have me to do?" It is the Lord's purpose that His method of healing without drugs shall be brought into prominence in every large city through our medical institutions. God invests with holy dignity those who go forth in His power to heal the sick. Let the light shine forth farther and still farther, in every place to which it is possible to obtain entrance. Satan will make the work as difficult as possible, but divine power will attend all true-hearted workers. Guided by our heavenly Father's hand, let us go forward, improving every opportunity to extend the work of God. —*Medical Ministry, 325.*

Men of stamina are wanted, men who will not wait to have their way smoothed and every obstacle removed, men who will inspire with fresh zeal the flagging efforts of dispirited workers, men whose hearts are warm with Christian love and whose hands are strong to do their Master's work. —*The Ministry of Healing, 497.*

Chapter 3

Ways of Working

Ministering to Body and Soul

Christ's servants are to follow His example. As He went from place to place, He comforted the suffering and healed the sick. Then He placed before them the great truths in regard to His kingdom. This is the work of His followers. As you relieve the sufferings of the body, you will find ways for ministering to the wants of the soul. You can point to the uplifted Saviour and tell of the love of the great Physician, who alone has power to restore. —*Christ's Object Lessons, 233, 234.*

A Door of Entrance to the Cities

Henceforth medical missionary work is to be carried forward with an earnestness with which it has never yet been carried. This work is the door through which the truth is to find entrance to the large cities. —*Testimonies for the Church 9:167.*

Organize for Harmonious Action

To those who have been engaged in this work I would say, Continue to work with tact and ability. Arouse your associates to work under some name whereby they may be organized to co-operate in harmonious action. Get the young men and women in the churches to work.

Combine medical missionary work with the proclamation of the third angel's message. Make regular, organized efforts to lift the church members out of the dead level in which they have been for years. Send out into the churches workers who will live the principles of health reform. Let those be sent who can see the necessity of self-denial in appetite, or they will be a snare to the church. See if the breath of life will not then come into your churches. A new element needs to be brought into the work. God's people must realize their great need and peril and take up the work that lies nearest to them. —

Testimonies for the Church 6:267.

The Church a Training School

The church of Christ is organized for service. Its watchword is ministry. Its members are soldiers, to be trained for conflict under the Captain of their salvation. Christian ministers, physicians, teachers, have a broader work than many have recognized. They are not only to minister to the people, but to teach them to minister. They should not only give instruction in right principles, but educate their hearers to impart these principles. Truth that is not lived, that is not imparted, loses its life-giving power, its healing virtue. Its blessing can be retained only as it is shared.

The monotony of our service for God needs to be broken up. Every church member should be engaged in some line of service for the Master. Some cannot do so much as others, but everyone should do his utmost to roll back the tide of disease and distress that is sweeping over our world. Many would be willing to work if they were taught how to begin. They need to be instructed and encouraged.

Every church should be a training school for Christian workers. Its members should be taught how to give Bible readings, how to conduct and teach Sabbath school classes, how best to help the poor and to care for the sick, how to work for the unconverted. There should be schools of health, cooking schools, and classes in various lines of Christian help work. There should not only be teaching, but actual work under experienced instructors. Let the teachers lead the way in working among the people and others, uniting with them, will learn from their example. One example is worth more than many precepts. —*The Ministry of Healing, 148, 149.*

The Need for Consecrated Nurses

Earnest, devoted young people are needed to enter the work of God as nurses. As these young men and women use conscientiously the knowledge they gain, they will increase in capability and become better and better qualified to be the Lord's helping hand. They may become successful missionaries, pointing souls to the Lamb of God, who taketh away the sin of the world, and who can save both soul and body.

The Lord wants wise men and women, acting in the capacity of nurses, to comfort and help the sick and suffering. Oh, that all who are afflicted could be ministered to by Christlike physicians and nurses who could help them to place their weary, pain-racked bodies in the care of the great Healer, in faith looking to Him for restoration.

Every sincere Christian bows to Jesus as the true Physician of souls. When He stands by the bedside of the afflicted, there will be many not only converted, but healed. If through judicious ministration the patient is led to give his soul to Christ and to bring his thoughts into obedience to the will of God, a great victory is gained. —*The Review and Herald, May 9, 1912.*

Serve With Sanctified Understanding

To those who go out to do medical missionary work, I would say, Serve the Lord Jesus Christ with sanctified understanding, in connection with the ministers of the gospel and the Great Teacher. He who has given you your commission will give you skill and understanding as you consecrate yourselves to His service, engaging diligently in labor and study, doing your best to bring relief to the sick and suffering. —*Counsels on Health, 539.*

Nothing but earnest, wholehearted labor will avail in the saving of souls. We are to make our everyday duties acts of devotion, constantly increasing in usefulness because we see our work in the light of eternity. —*Letter 43, 1902.*

Medical Missions in Every City

Intemperance has filled our world, and medical missions should be established in every city. By this I do not mean that expensive institutions should be established, calling for a large outlay of means. These missions are to be conducted in such a way that they will not be a heavy drain on the cause; and their work is to prepare the way for the establishment of present truth. Medical missionary work should have its representatives in every place in connection with the establishment of our churches. The relief of bodily suffering opens the way for the healing of the sin-sick soul. —*Medical Ministry, 322.*

In every city where we have a church, there is need of a place where treatments can be given.... A place should be provided where treatments may be given for common ailments. The building might be inelegant and even rude, but it should be furnished with facilities for giving simple treatments. —*Testimonies for the Church 6:113.*

The City Mission and Training School

A well-balanced work can be carried on best when a training school for Bible workers is in progress. While the public meetings are being held, connected with this training school or city mission should be experienced laborers of deep spiritual understanding, who can give the Bible workers daily instruction, and who can also unite wholeheartedly in the general public effort being put forth. And as men and women are converted to the truth, those standing at the head of the city mission should, with much prayer, show these new converts how to experience the power of the truth in their lives. This united effort on the part of all the workers would be as a nail driven in a sure place. —*Testimonies for the Church 9:111, 112.*

Training Under Competent Leaders

More attention should be given to training and educating missionaries with a special reference to work in the cities. Each company of workers should be under the direction of a competent leader, and it should ever be kept before them that they are to be missionaries in the highest sense of the term. Such systematic labor, wisely conducted, would produce blessed results. —*Medical Ministry, 301.*

From the instruction that the Lord has given me from time to time, I know that there should be workers who make medical evangelistic tours among the towns and villages. Those who do this work will gather a rich harvest of souls from both the higher and lower classes. The way for this work is best prepared by the efforts of the faithful canvasser.

Many will be called into the field to labor from house to house, giving Bible readings, and praying with those who are interested. —*Testimonies for the Church 9:172.*

Laboring as God's Helping Hand

Our work has been marked out for us by our heavenly Father. We are to take our Bibles and go forth to warn the world. We are to be God's helping hand in saving souls. We are to be channels through which His love is day by day to flow to the perishing. The realization of the great work in which he has the privilege of taking part ennobles and sanctifies the true worker. He is filled with the faith that works by love and purifies the soul. Nothing is drudgery to the one who submits to the will of God. "Doing it unto the Lord" is the thought that throws a charm over the work that God gives him to do. —*Letter 43, 1902.*

Self-supporting Workers

The Macedonian cry is coming from every quarter. Shall men go to the "regular lines" to see whether they will be permitted to labor, or shall they go out and work as best they can, depending on their own abilities and on the help of the Lord, beginning in a humble way and creating an interest in the truth in places in which nothing has been done to give the warning message?

The Lord has encouraged those who have started out on their own responsibility to work for Him, their hearts filled with love for souls ready to perish. A true missionary spirit will be imparted to those who seek earnestly to know God and Jesus Christ, whom He hath sent. The Lord lives and reigns. Young men, go forth into the places to which you are directed by the Spirit of the Lord. Work with your hands, that you may be self-supporting, and as you have opportunity proclaim the message of warning. —*Medical Ministry, 321-322.*

Where are the men who will work and study and agonize in prayer as did Christ? We are not to confine our efforts to a few places. "When they persecute you in this city, flee ye into another." Let Christ's plan be followed. He was ever watching for opportunities to engage in personal labor, ever ready to interest and draw men to a study of the Scriptures. He labored patiently for men who had not an intelligent knowledge of what is truth. While we are not awake to the situation, and while much time is consumed in planning how to reach perishing souls, Satan is busy devising and blocking the way. —*Medical Ministry, 303.*

Hygienic Restaurants as Missionary Centers

The opening of hygienic restaurants is a work that God would have done in the cities. If wisely conducted, these restaurants will be missionary centers. Those working in them should have at hand publications on health and temperance topics and on other phases of gospel truth, to give to those coming for meals. —*Manuscript 114, 1902.*

To Supply Spiritual Food

The workers in our restaurants are to prepare for the future immortal life. Let them acquire the power and tact to prepare spiritual food for the souls of men and women in these large cities. Watch for souls as they that must give an account. The cities are to be warned, and these young men and young women should remember that time is precious. The world is increasing in wickedness as in the days of Noah. —*Letter 279, 1905.*

Results of Consecrated Effort

All missionary successes have been gained by consecrated effort. By God's ordained means we can work successfully, meeting and surmounting obstacles, standing steadfastly under Christ's banner, refusing to fail or become discouraged. —*Special Testimonies, Series B, No. 2, p. 19.*

The experience of apostolic days will come to us if men will be worked by the Holy Spirit. The Lord will withdraw His blessing where selfish interests are indulged; but He will put His people in possession of good throughout the world, it they will unselfishly use their ability for the uplifting of humanity. His work is to be a sign of His benevolence, a sign that will win the confidence of the world and bring in resources for the advancement of the gospel. —*Special Testimonies, Series B, No. 1, p. 20.*

As a people who are doing a special work for this time, we are now to manifest a faith that will have a convincing power. —*Letter 82, 1907.*

Chapter 4

Christian Help Work

Ministering to Those in Need

There is a work to be done by our churches that few have any idea of. "I was an hungred," Christ says, "and ye gave me meat; I was thirsty, and ye gave me drink; I was a stranger, and ye took me in; naked, and ye clothed me; I was sick, and ye visited me;

I was in prison, and ye came unto me." We shall have to give of our means to support laborers in the harvest field, and we shall rejoice in the sheaves gathered in. But while this is right, there is a work, as yet untouched, that must be done. The mission of Christ was to heal the sick, encourage the hopeless, bind up the brokenhearted. This work of restoration is to be carried on among the needy, suffering ones of humanity. God calls not only for your benevolence, but your cheerful countenance, your hopeful words, the grasp of your hand. Relieve some of God's afflicted ones. Some are sick, and hope has departed. Bring back the sunlight to them. There are souls who have lost their courage; speak to them, pray for them. There are those who need the bread of life. Read to them from the Word of God. There is a soul sickness no balm can reach, no medicine heal. Pray for these, and bring them to Jesus Christ. And in all your work, Christ will be present to make impressions upon human hearts.

This is the kind of medical missionary work to be done. Bring the sunshine of the Sun of Righteousness into the room of the sick and suffering. Teach the inmates of the poor homes how to cook. "He shall feed his flock like a shepherd," with temporal and spiritual food. —*Manuscript 105, 1898.*

Carrying the Gospel to the Poor

The poverty of the people to whom we are sent is not to prevent us from working for them. Christ came to this earth to walk and work among the poor and suffering. They received the greatest share of His attention. And today, in the person of His children, He visits the poor and needy, relieving woe and alleviating suffering.

Take away suffering and need, and we should have no way of understanding the mercy and love of God, no way of knowing the compassionate, sympathetic heavenly Father. Never does the gospel put on an aspect of greater loveliness than when it is brought to the most needy and destitute regions. Then it is that its light shines forth with the clearest radiance and the greatest power. Truth from the Word of God enters the hovel of the peasant; rays from the Sun of Righteousness light up the rude cottage of the poor, bringing gladness to the sick and suffering. Angels of God are there, and the simple faith shown makes the crust of bread and the cup of water a banquet. The sin-pardoning Saviour welcomes the poor and ignorant, and gives them to eat of the bread that comes down from heaven. They drink of the water of life. Those who have been loathed and abandoned are through faith and pardon raised to the dignity of sons and daughters of God. Lifted above the world, they sit in heavenly places in Christ. They may have no earthly treasure, but they have found the Pearl of great price. —*Testimonies for the Church 7:226, 227.*

Helping the Helpless

The work of gathering in the needy, the oppressed, the suffering, the destitute, is the very work which every church that believes the truth for this time should long since have been doing. We are to show the tender sympathy of the Samaritan, ... feeding the hungry, bringing the poor that are cast out to our homes, gathering from God every day grace and strength that will enable us to reach to the very depths of human misery and help those who cannot possibly help themselves. In doing this work we have a favorable opportunity to set forth Christ the Crucified One.

Every church member should feel it his special duty of labor for those living in his neighborhood. Study how you can best help those who take no interest in religious things. As you visit your friends and neighbors, show an interest in their spiritual as well as in their temporal welfare. Present Christ as a sin-pardoning Saviour. Invite your neighbors to your home, and read with them from the precious Bible and from books that explain its truths. This, united with simple songs and fervent prayers, will touch their hearts. Let church members educate themselves to do this work. —*Testimonies for the Church*

6:276.

A Witness to the Power of Christianity

Christ has placed upon His church a sacred charge, the fulfilling of which calls for self-denial at every step. When those who believe in Him are seen lifting the cross and bearing it after Him in the path of self-denial, willingly doing all in their power to bring blessing to those for whom Christ died, witness will be borne to the power of Christianity; and in the hearts of many, now unbelievers, will spring up faith in Him who gave His life to save a guilty world from eternal ruin. —*Letter 43, 1903.*

Need of Greater Faith

As believers in Christ we need greater faith. We need to be more fervent in prayer. Many wonder why their prayers are so lifeless, their faith so feeble and wavering, their Christian experience so dark and uncertain. "Have we not fasted," they say, "and walked mournfully before the Lord of hosts?" In the fifty-eighth chapter of Isaiah Christ has shown how this condition of things may be changed. He says: "Is not this the fast that I have chosen? to loose the bands of wickedness, to undo the heavy burdens, and to let the oppressed go free, and that ye break every yoke? Is it not to deal thy bread to the hungry, and that thou bring the poor that are cast out to thy house? when thou seest the naked, that thou cover him; and that thou hide not thyself from thine own flesh?" Verses 6, 7. This is the recipe that Christ has prescribed for the fainthearted, doubting, trembling soul. Let the sorrowful ones, who walk mournfully before the Lord, arise and help someone who needs help.

Every church is in need of the controlling power of the Holy Spirit; and now is the time to pray for it. But in all God's work for man He plans that man shall co-operate with Him. To this end the Lord calls upon the church to have a higher piety, a more just sense of duty, a clearer realization of their obligations to their Creator. He calls upon them to be a pure, sanctified, working people. And the Christian help work is one means of bringing this about, for the Holy Spirit communicates with all who are doing God's service. —*Testimonies for the Church 6:266, 267.*

Keeping Our Souls Alive

There is a great variety of work, adapted to different minds and varied capabilities. In the day of God not one will be excused for being shut up to his own selfish interests. And it is by working for others that you will keep your own souls alive.

Do you shrink from this work because there is a cross connected with it? Remember that self must be denied if you would win Christ. Earnest, unselfish effort will garner sheaves for Jesus. The humble worker who obediently responds to the call of God, may be sure of receiving divine assistance. The Lord is a mighty helper. If the workers will rely wholly upon Him, He will accomplish a great work through them. —*Historical Sketches, 182.*

Use Your Humble Talent

Begin to do medical missionary work with the conveniences which you have at hand. You will find that thus the way will open for you to hold Bible readings. The heavenly Father will place you in connection with those who need to know how to treat their sick ones. Put into practice what you know regarding the treatment of disease. Thus suffering will be relieved, and you will have opportunity to break the bread of life to starving souls.

It is the duty of Christians to convince the world that the religion of Christ disrobes the soul of the garments of heaviness and mourning and clothes it with joy and gladness. Those who receive Christ as a sin-pardoning Saviour are clothed with His garments of light. He takes away their sin and imparts to them His righteousness. Their joy is full.

Who have better right than Christians to sing songs of rejoicing? Have they not the expectation of being members of the royal family, children of the heavenly King? Is not the gospel good tidings of great joy? When the promises of God are freely and fully accepted, heaven's brightness is brought into the life....

An Expression of Gratitude

He who is truly converted will be so filled with the love of God that he will long to impart to others the joy that he himself possesses. The Lord desires His church to hold forth to the world the beauty of holiness. She is to demonstrate the power of Christian religion. Heaven is to be reflected in the character of the Christian. The song of gratitude and praise is to be heard by those in darkness. For the good tidings of the gospel, for its promises and assurances, we are to express our gratitude by seeking to do others good. The doing of medical missionary work brings rays of heavenly brightness to wearied, perplexed, suffering souls. It is as a fountain opened for the wayworn, thirsty traveler. At every work of mercy, every work of love, angels of God are present. Those who live nearest to heaven will reflect the brightness of the Sun of Righteousness. —*Manuscript 55, 1901.*

The duty and delight of all service is to uplift Christ before the people. This is the end of all true labor. Let Christ appear; let self be hidden behind Him. This is self-sacrifice that is of worth. —*Testimonies for the Church 9:147.*

All around us are doors open for service. We should become acquainted with our neighbors, and seek to draw them to Christ. As we do this, He will approve and co-operate with us. —*Testimonies for the Church 9:171.*

Chapter 5

A Complete Ministry

Christ, Our Example

Christ has given us an example. He taught from the Scriptures the gospel truths, and He also healed the afflicted ones who came to Him for relief. He was the greatest physician the world ever knew, and yet He combined with His healing work the imparting of soul-saving truth.

The Physician as an Evangelist

And thus should our physicians labor. They are doing the Lord's work when they labor as evangelists, giving instruction as to how the soul may be healed by the Lord Jesus. Every physician should know how to pray in faith for the sick, as well as to administer the proper treatment. At the same time he should labor as one of God's ministers, to teach repentance and conversion, and the salvation of soul and body. Such a combination of labor will broaden his experience and greatly enlarge his influence.

One thing I know, the greatest work for our physicians is to get access to the people of the world in the right way. There is a world perishing in sin, and who will take up the work in our cities? The greatest physician is the one who walks in the footsteps of Jesus Christ. —*Counsels on Health, 544.*

The Minister as a Medical Missionary

The minister will often be called upon to act the part of a physician. He should have a training that will enable him to administer the simpler remedies for the relief of suffering. Ministers and Bible workers should prepare themselves for this line of work; for in doing it, they are following the example of Christ. They should be as well prepared by education and practice to combat disease of the body as they are to heal the sin-sick soul by pointing to the great Physician. They are fulfilling the commission which Christ gave to the twelve and afterwards to the seventy: "Into whatsoever city ye enter ... heal the sick that are therein, and say unto them, The kingdom of God is come nigh unto you." Christ stands by their side, as ready to heal the sick as when He was on this earth in person. —*Medical Ministry, 253.*

To take people right where they are, whatever their position, whatever their condition, and help them in every way possible, this is gospel ministry. It may be necessary for ministers to go into the homes of the sick and say, "I am ready to help you, and I will do the best I can. I am not a physician, but I am a minister, and I like to minister to the sick and afflicted." Those who are sick in body are nearly always sick in soul, and when the soul is sick, the body is made sick. —*Medical Ministry, 238.*

Teaching Health Principles

All gospel workers should know how to give the simple treatments that do so much to relieve pain and remove disease. —*Ministry of Healing, 146.*

Every gospel worker should feel that the giving of instruction in the principles of healthful living is a part of his appointed work. Of this work there is great need, and the world is open for it. —*The Ministry of Healing, 147.*

The Missionary Nurse

There are many lines of work to be carried forward by the missionary nurse. There are openings for well-trained nurses to go among families and seek to awaken an interest in the truth. In almost every community there are large numbers who do not attend any religious service. If they are reached by the gospel, it must be carried to their homes. Often the relief of their physical needs is the only avenue by which they can be approached. As missionary nurses care for the sick and relieve the distress of the poor, they will find many opportunities to pray with them, to read to them from God's Word, to speak of the Saviour. They can pray with and for the helpless ones who have not strength of will to control the appetites that passion has degraded. They can bring a ray of hope into the lives of the defeated and disheartened. Their unselfish love, manifested in acts of disinterested kindness, will make it easier for these suffering ones to believe in the love of Christ.

Many have no faith in God and have lost confidence in man. But they appreciate acts of sympathy and helpfulness. As they see one with no inducement of earthly praise or compensation coming to their homes, ministering to the sick, feeding the hungry, clothing the naked, comforting the sad, and tenderly pointing all to Him of whose love and pity the human worker is but the messenger- as they see this, their hearts are touched. Gratitude springs up, faith is kindled. They see that God cares for them, and as His Word is opened they are prepared to listen. —*The Review and Herald, May 9, 1912.*

There should be companies organized and educated most thoroughly to work as nurses, as evangelists, as ministers, as canvassers, as gospel students, to perfect a character after the divine similitude. To prepare to receive the higher education in the school above is now to be our purpose....

Do Not Wait

Workers-gospel medical missionaries-are needed now. You cannot afford to spend years in preparation. Soon doors now open to the truth will be forever closed. Carry the message now. Do not wait, allowing the enemy to take possession of the fields now open before you. Let little companies go forth to do the work to which Christ appointed His disciples. Let them labor as evangelists, scattering our publications, and talking of the truth to those they meet. Let them pray for the sick, ministering to their necessities, not with drugs, but with nature's remedies, and teaching them how to regain health and avoid disease. —*Testimonies for the Church 9:171, 172.*

Chapter 6

Teaching Health Principles

Extent of the Work

God has qualified His people to enlighten the world. He has entrusted them with faculties by which they are to extend His work until it shall encircle the globe. In all parts of the earth, they are to establish sanitariums, schools, publishing houses, and kindred facilities for the accomplishment of His work.

The closing message of the gospel is to be carried to "every nation, and kindred, and tongue, and people." Revelation 14:6. In foreign countries many enterprises for the advancement of this message must yet be begun and carried forward. The opening of hygienic restaurants and treatment rooms, and the establishment of sanitariums for the care of the sick and the suffering, is just as necessary in Europe as in America. In many lands medical missions are to be established to act as God's helping hand in ministering to the afflicted. —*Testimonies for the Church 7:51.*

Educate, Educate, Educate

We must educate, educate, educate, pleasantly and intelligently. We must preach the truth, pray the truth, and live the truth, bringing it, with its gracious, health-giving influences within the reach of those who know it not. As the sick are brought into touch with the Life-giver, their faculties of mind and body will be renewed. But in order for this to be, they must practice self-denial and be temperate in all things. Thus only can they be saved from physical and spiritual death and restored to health. —*Medical Ministry, 262.*

If we would elevate the moral standard in any country where we may be called to go, we must begin by correcting their physical habits. Virtue of character depends upon the right action of the powers of the mind and body. —*Counsels on Health, 505.*

Teach Skillfully

Wherever the truth is carried, the people should be given instruction in regard to the preparation of healthful foods. God desires that in every place the people should be taught by skillful teachers how to utilize wisely the products that they can raise or readily obtain in their section of the country. Thus the poor, as well as those in better circumstances, can be taught to live healthfully.

All the way along from the beginning, we have found it necessary to educate, educate, educate. God desires us to continue to educate the people. We are not to neglect this work because of the effect we may fear it will have on the sale of goods manufactured in our health food factories. This is not the most important matter. Our work is to show the people how they can obtain and prepare wholesome food, how they can co-operate with God in restoring in themselves His image. —*Letter 135, 1902.*

A Continual Reform Essential

Reform, continual reform, must be kept before the people, and by our example we must enforce our teachings. True religion and the laws of health go hand in hand. It is impossible to work for the salvation of men and women without presenting to them the need of breaking away from sinful gratifications, which destroy the health, debase the soul, and prevent divine truth from impressing the mind. Men and women must be taught to take a careful review of every habit and every practice, and at once put away those things that cause an unhealthy condition of the body, and thus cast a dark shadow over the mind. —*Counsels on Health, 445.*

Those who act as teachers are to be intelligent in regard to disease and its causes, understanding that every action of the human agent should be in perfect harmony with the laws of life. The light God has given on health reform is for our salvation and the salvation of the world. Men and women should be informed in regard to the human habitation, fitted up by our Creator as His dwelling place, and over which He desires us to be faithful stewards. "For ye are the temple of the living God; as God hath said, I will dwell in them, and walk in them; and I will be their God, and they shall be my people." —*The Review and Herald, November 12, 1901.*

Responsibility of Those Who Have Light

There are but few as yet who are aroused sufficiently to understand how much their habits of diet have to do with their health, their characters, their usefulness in this world, and their eternal destiny. I saw that it is the duty of those who have received the light from Heaven, and have realized the benefit of walking in it, to manifest a greater interest for those who are still suffering for want of knowledge. Sabbathkeepers who are looking for the soon appearing of their Saviour should be the last to manifest a lack of interest in this great work of reform. Men and women must be instructed, and ministers and people should feel that the burden of the work rests upon them to agitate the subject, and urge it home upon others. —*Testimonies for the Church 1:488, 489.*

Thousands Eager to Learn

Gospel workers should be able also to give instruction in the principles of healthful living. There is sickness everywhere, and most of it might be prevented by attention to the laws of health. The people need to see the bearing of health principles upon their well-being, both for this life and for the life to come....

Thousands need and would gladly receive instruction concerning the simple methods of treating the sick—methods that are taking the place of the use of poisonous drugs. There is great need of instruction in regard to dietetic reform. Wrong habits of eating and the use of unhealthful food are in no small degree responsible for the intemperance and crime and wretchedness that curse the world.

In teaching health principles keep before the mind the great object of reform, that its purpose is to secure the highest development of body and mind and soul. —*The Ministry of Healing, 146.*

The Public to Be Deeply Stirred

All are bound by the most sacred obligations to God to heed the sound philosophy and genuine experience which he is now giving them in reference to health reform. He designs that the great subject of health reform shall be agitated, and the public mind deeply stirred to investigate; for it is impossible for men and women, with all their sinful, health-destroying, brain-enervating habits, to discern sacred truth, through which they are to be sanctified, refined, elevated, and made fit for the society of heavenly angels in the kingdom of glory. —*Testimonies for the Church 3:162.*

Health Talks to Be Given

The Lord has presented before me that many, many will be rescued from physical, mental, and moral degeneracy through the practical influence of health reform. Health talks will be given, publications will be multiplied. The principles of health reform will be received with favor; and many will be enlightened. The influences that are associated with health reform will commend it to the judgment of all who want light; and they will advance step by step to receive the special truths for this time. Thus truth and righteousness will meet together. —*Testimonies for the Church 6:378, 379.*

Physiology to Be Taught

So closely is health related to our happiness that we cannot have the latter without the former. A practical knowledge of the science of human life is necessary in order to glorify God in our bodies. It is therefore of the highest importance, that among the studies selected for childhood, physiology should occupy the first place. How few know anything about the structure and functions of their own bodies, and of nature's laws! Many are drifting about without knowledge, like a ship at sea without compass or anchor; and what is more, they are not interested to learn how to keep their bodies in a healthy condition and prevent disease. —*Counsels on Health, 38.*

Represented by Advance Principles

Satan is constantly urging men to accept his principles, and thus he is seeking to counterwork the work of God. He is constantly representing the chosen people of God as a deluded people. He is an accuser of the brethren, and his accusing power he is constantly using against those who work righteousness. The Lord desires through His people to answer Satan's charges by showing the result of obedience to right principles. He desires our health institutions to stand as witnesses for the truth. They are to give character to the work which must be carried forward in these last days in restoring man through a reformation of the habits, appetites, and passions. Seventh-day Adventists are to be represented to the world by the advance principles of health reform which God has given us. —*Medical Ministry, 187.*

Education Better Than Miraculous Healing

Some have asked me, "Why should we have sanitariums? Why should we not, like Christ, pray for the sick, that they may be healed miraculously?" I have answered, "Suppose we were able to do this in all cases; how many would appreciate the healing? Would those who were healed become health reformers, or continue to be health destroyers?"

Jesus Christ is the Great Healer, but He desires that by living in conformity with His laws, we may co-operate with Him in the recovery and the maintenance of health. Combined with the work of healing there must be an imparting of knowledge of how to resist temptations. Those who come to our sanitariums should be aroused to a sense of their own responsibility to work in harmony with the God of truth.

We cannot heal. We cannot change the diseased conditions of the body. But it is our part, as medical missionaries, as workers together with God, to use the means that He has provided. Then we should pray that God will bless these agencies. We do believe in a God; we believe in a God who hears and answers prayer. He has said, "Ask, and ye shall receive; seek, and ye shall find; knock, and it shall be opened unto you." —*Medical Ministry, 13.*

When Prayer for Healing Is Presumption

Many have expected that God would keep them from sickness merely because they have asked Him to do so. But God did not regard their prayers, because their faith was not made perfect by works. God will not work a miracle to keep those from sickness who have no care for themselves, but are continually violating the laws of health and make no efforts to prevent disease. When we do all we can on our part to have health, then may we expect that the blessed results will follow, and we can ask God in faith to bless our efforts for the preservation of health. He will then answer our prayer, if His name can be glorified thereby. But let all understand that they have a work to do. God will not work in a miraculous manner to preserve the health of persons who are taking a sure course to make themselves sick, by their careless inattention to the laws of health.

Those who will gratify their appetite, and then suffer because of their intemperance, and take drugs to relieve them, may be assured that God will not interpose to save health and life which are so recklessly periled. The cause has produced the effect. Many, as their last resort, follow the directions in the Word of God, and request the prayers of the elders of the church for their restoration to health. God does not see fit to answer prayers offered in behalf of such, for He knows that if they should be restored to health, they would again sacrifice it upon the altar of unhealthy appetite. —*Medical Ministry, 13, 14.*

Instruction in Diet by Evangelistic Workers

As a people we have been given the work of making known the principles of health reform. There are some who think that the question of diet is not of sufficient importance to be included in their evangelistic work. But such make a great mistake. God's Word declares, "Whether therefore ye eat, or drink, or whatsoever ye do, do all to the glory of God." The subject of temperance, in all its bearings, has an important place in the work of salvation. —*Testimonies for the Church 9:112.*

A Knowledge of Healthful Cookery

One reason why many have become discouraged in practicing health reform is that they have not learned how to cook so that proper food, simply prepared, would supply the place of the diet to which they have been accustomed. They become disgusted with the poorly prepared dishes, and next we hear them say that they have tried the health reform and cannot live in that way. Many attempt to follow out meager instructions in health reform and make such sad work that it results in injury to digestion, and in discouragement to all concerned in the attempt. You profess to be health reformers, and for this very reason you should become good cooks. Those who can avail themselves of the advantages of properly conducted hygienic cooking schools will find it a great benefit both in their own practice and in teaching others. —*Counsels on Health, 450, 451.*

Often health reform is made health deform by the unpalatable preparation of food. The lack of knowledge regarding healthful cookery must be remedied before health reform is a success. —*Medical Ministry, 270.*

Simplicity in Cooking

Greater efforts should be put forth to educate the people in the principles of health reform. More cooking schools should be established, and some should labor from house to house giving instruction in the art of cooking wholesome food. Parents and their children should learn to cook more simply than is usually done. The preparation of so many varied and complex dishes so absorbs the time and attention of many that they are disqualified to teach the truth as it is in Jesus. —*Letter 279, 1905.*

Many of the views held by Seventh-day Adventists differ widely from those held by the world in general. Those who advocate an unpopular truth should, above all others, seek to be consistent in their own life. They should not try to see how different they can be from others, but how near they can come to those whom they wish to influence, that they may help them to the positions they themselves so highly prize. Such a course will commend the truths they hold.

Those who are advocating a reform in diet should, by the provision they make for their own table, present the advantages of hygiene in the best light. They should so exemplify its principles as to commend it to the judgment of candid minds....

Decision Without Narrow Conceit

But no one should permit opposition or ridicule to turn him from the work of reform, or cause him to lightly regard it. He who is imbued with the spirit which actuated Daniel will not be narrow or conceited, but he will be firm and decided in standing for the right. In all his associations, whether with his brethren or with others, he will not swerve from principle, while at the same time he will not fail to manifest a noble, Christlike patience. —*Christian Temperance and Bible Hygiene, 55.*

Chapter 7

The Temperance Work

Revive the Temperance Work

Messengers should be appointed who can present the Word of God from city to city upon the subject of temperance. —*Manuscript 52, 1900.*

The tame way in which the temperance question is being handled by our people is not in harmony with the necessities of the times. The work of making known our belief in matters of temperance should now be entered into most heartily. —*Letter 302, 1907.*

In the advocacy of the cause of temperance, our efforts are to be multiplied. The subject of Christian temperance should find a place in our sermons in every city where we labor. Health reform in all its bearings is to be presented before the people, and special efforts made to instruct the youth, the middle-aged, and the aged in the principles of Christian living. Let this phase of the message be revived, and let the truth go forth as a lamp that burneth. —*Manuscript 61, 1909.*

An Opportunity for Young Men

Will young men now humble their hearts before God and give themselves to His service? Will they not accept the holy trust, and become light-bearers to a world ready to be consumed by the wrath of an offended God?

The use of intoxicating drink, which dethrones reason, and tobacco, which clouds the brain and poisons the life current, is increasing. Are young men prepared to lift their voices in the cause of temperance and show its bearing upon Christianity? Will they engage in the holy war against appetite and lust?

Our artificial civilization encourages evils which are destroying sound principles. And the Lord is at the door. Where are the men who will go forth to the work, fully trusting in God, ready to do and to dare?

God calls, "Son, go work today in my vineyard." God will make the young men of today heaven's chosen repositories, to present before the people truth in contrast with error and superstition, if they will give themselves to Him. May God roll the burden on strong young men, who have His Word abiding in them, and who will give the truth to others. —*Manuscript 134, 1898.*

Make Plain the Effects of Indulgence

It must be kept before the people that the right balance of the mental and moral powers depends in a great degree on the right conditions of the physical system. All narcotics and unnatural stimulants that enfeeble and degrade the physical nature tend to lower the tone of the intellect and morals. Intemperance lies at the foundation of the moral depravity of the world. By the indulgence of perverted appetite, man loses his power to resist temptation.

Temperance reformers have a work to do in educating the people in these lines. Teach them that health, character, and even life, are endangered by the use of stimulants, which excite the exhausted energies to unnatural, spasmodic action. —*The Ministry of Healing, 335.*

Many May Be Saved From Degradation

I have been shown that the medical missionary work will discover, in the very depths of degradation, men who once possessed fine minds, richest qualifications, who will be rescued by proper labor from their fallen condition. It is the truth as it is in Jesus that is to be brought before human minds after they have been sympathetically cared for and their physical necessities met. The Holy Spirit is working and co-operating with the human agencies that are laboring for such souls, and some will appreciate the foundation upon a rock for their religious faith.

There is to be no startling communication of strange doctrine to these subjects whom God loves and pities; but as they are helped physically by the medical missionary workers, the Holy Spirit co-operates with the minister of human agencies, to arouse the moral powers. The mental powers are awakened into activity, and these poor souls will, many of them, be saved in the kingdom of God. —*Medical Ministry, 242, 243.*

Pledging to Total Abstinence

The subject of temperance should be strongly presented, and a pledge to abstain from all intoxicating liquor and from tobacco should be presented. Habits of intemperance are preventing minds from discerning the importance of the truths which make men wise unto salvation. The brain must be cleared from the befogging influence of intoxicating liquor and tobacco, and then men will realize that Christ has died for their salvation. —*Letter 187, 1904.*

Responsibility of Parents

Often intemperance begins in the home. By the use of rich, unhealthful food the digestive organs are weakened, and a desire is created for food that is still more stimulating. Thus the appetite is educated to crave continually something stronger. The demand for stimulants becomes more frequent and more difficult to resist. The system becomes more or less filled with poison, and the more debilitated it becomes, the greater is the desire for these things. One step in the wrong direction prepares the way for another. Many who would not be guilty of placing on their table wine or liquor of any kind will load their table with food which creates such a thirst for strong drink that to resist the temptation is almost impossible. Wrong habits of eating and drinking destroy the health and prepare the way for drunkenness.

There would soon be little necessity for temperance crusades, if in the youth who form and fashion society, right principles in regard to temperance could be implanted. Let parents begin a crusade against intemperance at their own firesides, in the principles they teach their children to follow from infancy, and they may hope for success.

There is work for mothers in helping their children to form correct habits and pure tastes. Educate the appetite; teach the children to abhor stimulants. Bring your children up to have moral stamina to resist the evil that surrounds them. Teach them that they are not to be swayed by others, that they are not to yield to strong influences, but to influence others for good. —*The Ministry of Healing, 334, 335.*

A Clear Testimony Needed

Every church needs a clear, sharp testimony, giving the trumpet a certain sound. If we can arouse the moral sensibilities upon the subject of practicing temperance in all things, a very great victory will be gained. —*Manuscript 59, 1900.*

Moses preached a great deal on this subject, and the reason the people did not go through to the promised land was because of repeated indulgence of appetite. Nine tenths of the wickedness among the children of today is caused by intemperance in eating and drinking. Adam and Eve lost Eden through the indulgence of appetite, and we only regain it by the denial of the same. —*The Review and Herald, October 21, 1884.*

When temperance is presented as a part of the gospel, many will see their need of reform. They will see the evil of intoxicating liquors, and that total abstinence is the only platform on which God's people can conscientiously stand. As this instruction is given, the people will become interested in other lines of Bible study. —*Testimonies for the Church 7:75.*

As we near the close of time, we must rise higher and still higher on the question of health reform and Christian temperance, presenting it in a more positive and decided manner. We must strive continually to educate the people, not only by our words but by our practice. Precept and practice combined have a telling influence. —*Manuscript 87, 1908.*

Chapter 8

Co-operation Between Medical and Evangelistic Work

How to Reveal Christ

How shall we reveal Christ? I know of no better way ... than to take hold of the medical missionary work in connection with the ministry. —*Medical Ministry, 319.*

Christ gave a perfect representation of true godliness by combining the work of a physician and a minister, ministering to the needs of both body and soul, healing physical disease, and then speaking words that brought peace to the troubled heart. —*Counsels on Health, 528.*

To Advance Together

The gospel and the medical missionary work are to advance together. The gospel is to be bound up with the principles of true health reform. Christianity is to be brought into the practical life. Earnest, thorough reformatory work is to be done. True Bible religion is an outflowing of the love of God for fallen man. God's people are to advance in straightforward lines to impress the hearts of those who are seeking for truth, who desire to act their part aright in this intensely earnest age. We are to present the principles of health reform before the people, doing all in our power to lead men and women to see the necessity of these principles and to practice them. —*Testimonies for the Church 6:379.*

Combined Teaching and Healing

The Lord's people are to be one. There is to be no separation in His work. Christ sent out the twelve apostles and afterward the seventy disciples to preach the gospel and to heal the sick. (Matthew 10:7, 8.) And as they went forth preaching the kingdom of God, power was given them to heal the sick and cast out evil spirits. In God's work teaching and healing are never to be separated. —*Testimonies for the Church 8:165.*

The Advantages of Medical Workers

One who is a physician and a religious teacher will find a work to do that will result in the salvation of souls. The form of sound words in religious teaching, sustained by a "Thus saith the Lord," will have a saving influence. A physician can so express himself that he will be invited to speak before various companies, and will be received. As a teacher, a physician can watch his opportunities; for the Word of God is to go freely.

Those who will enter our large cities to labor as medical evangelists must begin their work in a very wise way. Angels of God will make the impression, and under the hallowed influence of the Holy Spirit, hearts will be touched. The words of the speaker bringing the form of sound doctrine into actual contact with the hearers will result in the saving of souls. —*Letter 4, 1910.*

Medical and Evangelistic Work Bound Together

When connected with other lines of gospel effort, medical missionary work is a most effective instrument by which the ground is prepared for the sowing of the seeds of truth, and the instrument also by which the harvest is reaped. Medical missionary work is the helping hand of the gospel ministry. So far as possible, it would be well for evangelical workers to learn how to minister to the necessities of the body as well as the soul; for in doing this, they are following the example of Christ. Intemperance has well-nigh filled the world with disease, and the ministers of the gospel cannot spend their time and strength in relieving all in need of help. The Lord has ordained that Christian physicians and nurses shall labor in connection with those who preach the Word. The medical missionary work is to be bound up with the gospel ministry. —*The Review and Herald, September 10, 1908.*

No Other Work So Successful

In new fields no work is so successful as medical missionary work. If our ministers would work earnestly to obtain an education in medical missionary lines, they would be far better fitted to do the work Christ did as a medical missionary. By diligent study and practice, they can become so well acquainted with the principles of health reform, that wherever they go they will be a great blessing to the people they meet. —*Medical Ministry, 239.*

The Minister, the Physician, and the Bible Worker

The gospel minister should preach the health principles, for these have been given of God as among the means needed to prepare a people perfect in character. Therefore, health principles have been given to us that as a people we might be prepared in both mind and body to receive the fullness of God's blessing. The medical missionary work has its place and part in this closing gospel work.

The Christian physician has a high calling. With his fuller knowledge of the human system and its laws, he is in a position to preach the gospel of salvation with much efficiency and power.

The first and chief object of the gospel and all that pertains to it is to seek and to save that which is lost. The ministry of the gospel, whether by the minister or the physician, is to reach out to man a helping hand wherever it is needed. It is to minister to the sick and suffering physically as well as to the sin-sick soul.

Here the gospel minister and the Christian physician unite, and the Bible worker in her visit from house to house as well. —*The Review and Herald, October 29, 1914.*

Ministers, do not confine your work to merely giving Bible instruction. Do practical work. Seek to restore the sick to health. This is true ministry. Remember that the restoration of the body prepares the way for the restoration of the soul. —*Medical Ministry, 240.*

There Must Be No Separation

No line is to be drawn between the genuine medical missionary work and the gospel ministry. These two must blend. They are not to stand apart as separate lines of work. They are to be joined in an inseparable union, even as the hand is joined to the body. Those in our institutions are to give evidence that they understand their part in the genuine gospel medical missionary work. A solemn dignity is to characterize genuine medical missionaries. They are to be men who understand and know God and the power of His grace. —*Letter 102, 1900.*

Successful evangelistic work can be done in connection with medical missionary work. It is as these lines of work are united that we may expect to gather the most precious fruit for the Lord. —*Medical Ministry, 26.*

The presenting of Bible principles by an intelligent physician will have great weight with many people. There is efficiency and power with one who can combine in his influence the work of a physician and of a gospel minister. His work commends itself to the good judgment of the people. —*Counsels on Health, 546.*

Education for Medical Missionary Work

The education of students in medical missionary lines is not complete unless they are trained to work in connection with the church and the ministry. —*Counsels on Health, 557.*

The medical missionary workers are to be purified, sanctified, ennobled. They are to rise to the highest point of excellence. They are to be molded and fashioned after the divine similitude. Then they will see that health reform and medical missionary work are to be bound up with the preaching of the gospel. —*Testimonies for the Church 8:168.*

Chapter 9

Equipment for Service

Study Health Principles

Let our people show that they have a living interest in medical missionary work. Let them prepare themselves for usefulness by studying the books that have been written for our instruction in these lines. These books deserve much more attention and appreciation than they have received. Much that is for the benefit of all to understand has been written for the special purpose of instruction in the principles of health. —*Testimonies for the Church 7:63.*

Our Sabbathkeeping families should keep their minds filled with helpful principles of health reform and other lines of truth, that they may be a help to their neighbors. Be practical missionaries. Gather up all the knowledge possible that will help to combat disease. This may be done by those who are diligent students.

But few can take a course of training in our medical institutions. But all can study our health literature and become intelligent on this important subject. —*Medical Ministry, 320.*

A Solemn Warning

Let the church arise and shine. Let every family practice self-denial, doing all they can to improve their own condition. Those who are truly on the Lord's side will be self-denying and self-sacrificing. They will eat and drink to the glory of God, refusing to corrupt soul and body by intemperance. Then the condition of the church will testify that her light has not been removed. But if church members do not act the part God has assigned them, the movement of health reform will go on without them, and it will be seen that God has removed their candlestick out of its place. Those who refuse to receive and practice the light will be left in the background. —*Manuscript 78, 1900.*

The Only Medium for Character Building

The body is the only medium through which the mind and the soul are developed for the upbuilding of character. Hence it is that the adversary of souls directs his temptations to the enfeebling and degrading of the physical powers. His success here means the surrender to evil of the whole being. The tendencies of our physical nature, unless under the dominion of a higher power, will surely work ruin and death. —*The Ministry of Healing, 130.*

Sinful indulgence defiles the body and unfits men for spiritual worship. He who cherishes the light which God has given him upon health reform has an important aid in the work of becoming sanctified through the truth and fitted for immortality. But if he disregards that light and lives in violation of natural law, he must pay the penalty; his spiritual powers are benumbed, and how can he perfect holiness in the fear of God? —*Christian Temperance and Bible Hygiene, 10.*

Humility and Love

By the sacrifice of Christ every provision has been made for believers to receive all things that pertain to life and godliness. God calls upon us to reach the highest standard of glory and virtue. The perfection of Christ's character makes it possible for us to gain perfection.

He who desires to rise to true greatness must walk humbly before God, not with a forced humility, but with a genuine sense of his own inefficiency and of God's greatness. He is to strive earnestly to make the soul temple a place where God delights to dwell.

He whose heart God touches is filled with a great love for those who have never heard the truth. Their condition impresses him with a sense of personal woe. Taking his life in his hand, he hurries away, a God-sent, God-inspired messenger, to do a work in which angels can co-operate. —*Manuscript 73, 1901.*

Meeting God at the Altar of Self-sacrifice

At the altar of self-sacrifice—the appointed place of meeting between God and the soul—we receive from the hand of God the celestial torch which searches the heart, revealing its great need of an abiding Christ.—*Manuscript 9, 1899.*

The completeness of Christian character is attained when the impulse to help and bless others springs constantly from within, when the sunshine of heaven fills the heart and is expressed in the countenance. —*Manuscript 108, 1899.*

The Highest Service

When men and women have formed characters which God can endorse, when their self-denial and self-sacrifice have been fully made, when they are ready for the final test, ready to be introduced into God's family, what service will stand highest in the estimation of Him who gave Himself a willing offering to save a guilty race? What enterprise will be most dear to the heart of infinite love? What work will bring the greatest satisfaction and joy to the Father and the Son? The salvation of perishing souls. —*Manuscript 51, 1901.*

HARD TO FIND BOOKS AVAILABLE ON AMAZON
In Spanish versión also available
(EVERY BOOK IN BIG PRINT UNIQUE EDITION)

1. The Two Babylons (Big Print Edition) Hislop, $29.99.
2. The Book of Jesus Martyrs John Foxe, $29.99.
3. Daniel Uriah Smith, $22.99.
4. Revelation Uriah Smith, $27.99.
5. Thoughts from the Mount of Blessing with study guide, $19.99.
6. War of the Jews Flavius Josephus, $29.99.
7. Final Time Events Ellen White, $21.99.
8. Country Living Ellen White, $8.99
9. The Sanctified Life with study guide, $12.99.

BOOKS THAT WILL COMING SOON

1. Daniel: An Exhaustive Commentary of Ellen White.
2. Revelation: An Exhaustive Commentary of Ellen White.
3. The Third Angels Message, Alonzo T. Jones.
4. Genesis: An Exhaustive Commentary of Ellen White.
5. Steps to Christ with a study guide, Ellen White.
6. Last Day Events with a study guide, Ellen White.
7. Country living with a study guide, Ellen White.
8. Daniel and Revelation, Stephen N. Haskell.
9. Steps to Christ Word Search, Ellen White.
10. Healthful Living, Ellen White.

AND MORE...

Contact us for good bulk discounts and specials

kalhelministries21@gmail.com

www.ingramcontent.com/pod-product-compliance
Lightning Source LLC
Chambersburg PA
CBHW080901010526
44118CB00015B/2227